ADVOCATING FOR YOURSELF

BY ABBY COLICH

T0014699

BLUE OWL
BOOKS

TIPS FOR CAREGIVERS

Social and emotional learning (SEL) helps children manage emotions, learn how to feel empathy, create and achieve goals, and make good decisions. Strong lessons and support in SEL will help children establish positive habits in communication, cooperation, and decision-making. By incorporating SEL in early reading, children will learn the importance of communication and self-advocacy when working with others.

BEFORE READING

Talk to the reader about the importance of advocating for oneself in group work.

Discuss: Think of a time you needed to speak up for yourself. What did you do and say? Were you able to communicate your needs and wants?

AFTER READING

Talk about the importance of good communication and how it can help group work go smoothly.

Discuss: What does it mean to be assertive? Why is it important to speak up for yourself?

SEL GOAL

Children may have a difficult time understanding self-advocacy, especially when it comes to group work. Encourage readers to identify times they should speak up for themselves. Have children role-play and practice what they can say to advocate for themselves. Explain that when everyone advocates for him or herself and communicates well, everyone is equipped to do their best work.

TABLE OF CONTENTS

CHAPTER 1

FINDING YOUR STRENGTHS

You can learn a lot when you work in a group. It can help you reach **goals** and help you prepare to work with others when you grow up.

Learning to **advocate** for yourself is an important part of working in a group. Advocating for yourself means that you **communicate** your **opinions**, ideas, wants, and needs.

model

What are you good at? What do you like working on? When you know your strengths and interests, you'll know how you can best help your group succeed.

Theo likes to build things. He advocates for himself. He tells his group he can help build a model for their school project.

DON'T BRAG

Be **humble** when talking about your strengths. Don't talk about being better than others.

Knowing your strengths and weaknesses builds **self-awareness**. When you know what you can improve on, you can practice. This will help you build **confidence**.

Liz has a hard time speaking in front of others. She practices at home.

CHALLENGE YOURSELF

What if you don't get the job you want? What if there's a job nobody wants to do? **Challenge** yourself. Try to learn something new. Promise yourself that you will do the best you can.

CHAPTER 2

BEING ASSERTIVE

It is important to be **assertive** when working with others. This means being honest about your thoughts and feelings without being mean.

Jada writes out a group answer. Ella thinks it might be wrong. She is kind but assertive. "I'm worried that what you wrote isn't **accurate**," Ella says. She shares her ideas and reasons. Jada listens. Together, they rewrite the answer.

Sometimes others may try to do your part. It is important to stand up for yourself. Peter's job is decorating for a class party. Myra is worried things won't be ready in time. She starts doing Peter's job.

Peter is assertive. He says, "I will finish on time. I'll let you know if I need help, but I'd like to do it on my own." He stays calm and respectful.

DEALING WITH PROBLEMS

Speaking up for yourself and communicating well can help group projects go smoothly. But sometimes you may still have problems.

When things don't go your way, it's OK to be disappointed. Be **mindful** of your feelings, but try not to let them take over or get in the way of finishing your work. Take a break. Then speak up and ask for help if you need it.

Priya made a mistake on her group's science project. Now she might not finish it on time. She is upset and nervous. She tells Katelyn.

Katelyn says, "It's OK. Everyone makes mistakes. I messed up my team's poster last year, but everything worked out." Katelyn shows **empathy** by telling Priya she knows how she feels. She helps Priya fix the mistake.

OWN YOUR MISTAKES

Take **ownership** when you make a mistake. Admit your mistake. Then take actions to make it right.

Another way to advocate is to speak up for others. Or you can **encourage** them to speak up for themselves.

Delia notices that Alana is being left out of the group discussion. She reaches out to Alana. She encourages the other group members to include her.

CHAPTER 3

A group is strongest when everyone's opinions are heard and respected. When we advocate for ourselves, we can all do our best work.

GOALS AND TOOLS

GROW WITH GOALS

Advocating for yourself can help group projects and activities go smoothly. What can you do to better advocate for yourself?

Goal: Think of time you wish you had spoken up for yourself. Try to be aware the next time a similar situation occurs.

Goal: Think before you speak. Use words that clearly state your feelings and needs.

Goal: Help another team member advocate for him or herself. Help him or her communicate about what is bothering them or what they would like to see done differently.

WRITING REFLECTION

Advocating for yourself is important. Reflect on ways you've advocated for yourself in the past and how you can continue to in the future.

1. Write about a time you wish you would have advocated for yourself. What would you do differently now? How can you accept what happened and move on?

2. List some situations in which you might need to advocate for yourself. Write about what you might do in those situations.

3. Write down some phrases you can use when you need to be assertive. Practice saying them aloud or role-play them in your head.

GLOSSARY

accurate
Correct in details.

advocate
To act in support of a person, cause, or group.

assertive
Able to behave confidently and express oneself positively.

challenge
To test the skill or ability of.

communicate
To share information, ideas, or feelings with another person through language, eye contact, or gestures.

confidence
A belief that you have the necessary ability to succeed.

empathy
The ability to understand and be sensitive to the thoughts and feelings of others.

encourage
To give someone confidence, usually by using praise and support.

goals
Things you aim to do.

humble
Not thinking you are better or more important than other people.

mindful
A mentality achieved by focusing on the present moment and calmly recognizing and accepting your feelings, thoughts, and sensations.

opinions
Personal feelings or beliefs.

ownership
The state or fact of owning something.

self-awareness
The ability to recognize your own emotions and behaviors.

TO LEARN MORE

FACT SURFER

Finding more information is as easy as 1, 2, 3.

1. Go to www.factsurfer.com

2. Enter "**advocatingforyourself**" into the search box.

3. Choose your book to see a list of websites.

INDEX

Blue Owl Books are published by Jump!, 5357 Penn Avenue South, Minneapolis, MN 55419, www.jumplibrary.com

Copyright © 2022 Jump! International copyright reserved in all countries. No part of this book may be reproduced in any form without written permission from the publisher.

Library of Congress Cataloging-in-Publication Data
Names: Colich, Abby, author.
Title: Advocating for yourself / Abby Colich.
Description: Minneapolis: Jump!, Inc., 2022. | Series: Working together
Includes index. | Audience: Ages 7–10
Identifiers: LCCN 2021005513 (print)
LCCN 2021005514 (ebook)
ISBN 9781636901145 (hardcover)
ISBN 9781636901152 (paperback)
ISBN 9781636901169 (ebook)
Subjects: LCSH: Self-consciousness (Awareness)—Juvenile literature. | Assertiveness (Psychology)—Juvenile literature. | Honesty—Juvenile literature.
Self-confidence—Juvenile literature.
Classification: LCC BF311 .C5585 2022 (print)
LCC BF311 (ebook) | DDC 158.2—dc23
LC record available at https://lccn.loc.gov/2021005513
LC ebook record available at https://lccn.loc.gov/2021005514

Editor: Eliza Leahy
Designer: Molly Ballanger

Photo Credits: Krakenimages.com/Shutterstock, cover, 10; Odua Images/Shutterstock, 1, 11; StockImageFactory.com, 3; Jose Luis Pelaez Inc/Getty, 4; kali9/iStock, 5; FamVeld/Shutterstock, 6–7; YAKOBCHUK VIACHESLAV/Shutterstock, 8–9; kazkaz/Shutterstock, 12–13 (foreground); albkdb/iStock, 12–13 (background); Dmytro Zinkevych/Shutterstock, 14, 15; Prapat Aowsakorn/Shutterstock, 16–17; StockPlanets/iStock, 18–19; Robert Kneschke/Shutterstock, 20–21.

Printed in the United States of America at Corporate Graphics in North Mankato, Minnesota.